JACK O'L... SCARY HALLOWEEN

BY ROBERT KRAUS

A GOLDEN BOOK • NEW YORK

Western Publishing Company, Inc., Racine, Wisconsin 53404

It was Halloween night. Jack O'Lantern was going out trick-or-treating with his friends Gennifer Ghost and Shelly Skelly.

"Halloween is my favorite holiday," said Jack.
"Mine, too," said Gennifer.
"I like Thanksgiving," said Shelly. "That's when I can put some meat on my bones."
"Just what you need!" said Jack.

Jack, Gennifer, and Shelly knocked at the front door of the first house. *Knock, knock, knock.* Wendy Witch answered. "Scary Halloween!" said Wendy.

"Trick," said Jack.

"Or," said Gennifer.

"Treat!" said Shelly.

Wendy Witch gave them candied apples, and they
ran off laughing. Ha, ha, ha, ha, ha.

They knocked at the door of the next house.
Knock, knock, knock. Melvin Monster answered.
"Boo!" said Melvin.
   "Trick," said Jack.
   "Or," said Gennifer.
   "Treat!" said Shelly.

Melvin Monster gave them popcorn, and they ran off laughing. Hee, hee, hee, hee, hee.

They knocked at the door of the next house.
Rap, rap, rap. Bob Goblin answered. "Gobble, gobble,"
said Bob.

"Trick," said Jack.

"Or," said Gennifer.

"Treat!" said Shelly.

Bob Goblin gave them candy corn, and they ran off laughing. Yuk, yuk, yuk, yuk, yuk.

They knocked at the door of the next house.
Bang, bang, bang. The Creep From the Deep
answered. "Gurgle, gurgle," said the Creep.

"Trick-or-treat!" said Jack, Gennifer, and Shelly.

The Creep gave them saltwater taffy, and they ran
off laughing. Giggle, giggle, giggle, giggle, giggle.

They walked on until they came to a house on a hill.
"Who lives in that house?" said Jack.

"I'm not sure," said Gennifer.

"Maybe they're vampires," said Shelly. "Let's knock
at their door."

They knocked at the door of the house on the hill.
Knock, knock, knock. A pretty little girl answered.
"Hi," she said. "Happy Halloween!"
   "Eek!" shrieked Jack.
   "Help!" screamed Gennifer.
   "Bones, start traveling!" howled Shelly Skelly.

They ran all the way to Jack's house . . .

and hid under the bed. They didn't come out
until Christmas!